Carson-Dellosa Publishing
PROFESSIONAL RESOURCES

PREDICTABLE CHARTS:

Shared Writing for Kindergarten and First Grade

By

Dorothy P. Hall

and

Elaine Williams

Editor
Joey Bland

Artists
Courtney Bunn
Bill Neville
Julie Webb

Cover Design
Julie Webb

Table of Contents

A list of Professional References and a list of Children's Works Cited can be found on the inside back cover.

Predictable Charts

Introduction

This book is about a special kind of shared or interactive writing for kindergarten and early first grade called "predictable charts." This activity was first explained in an article written by Patricia Cunningham in 1979 titled, "Beginning Reading Without Readiness: Structured Language Experience." Dr. Cunningham taught all of her students at Wake Forest University, including undergraduates and practicing teachers enrolled in her graduate courses, how to use structured language so that all children could take part in language experience activities, regardless of their language skills. The teachers who implemented the strategy not only claimed that all of their students were able to take part in this activity, they also claimed that all the children felt like they could read and write. Kindergarten and first-grade teachers marveled at the success they had using structured language experience. They observed that all students in the class could dictate sentences using the predictable starter, and later the same students could read their sentences back to the teacher and class!

However, structured language experience was not used by a large number of kindergarten and first-grade teachers until Hall and Cunningham wrote a book for kindergarten teachers in 1997 and suggested using "predictable charts" as an activity. When teachers all over the country began writing predictable charts with their classes, they also discovered that *all* children could experience success with reading and writing regardless of their literacy levels. The multilevel nature of these charts, combined with the success all children experience as they write and read these charts have caused the predictable chart strategy to grow in popularity. Predictable charts now have a permanent place as emergent literacy activities.

Language experience (Russell Stauffer, 1970; Roach Van Allen, 1964) is a writing approach to teaching reading. When using the language experience approach, teachers spend time taking dictation from individual children and helping them learn to read their dictation. Language experience advocates believed children would be able to read their dictation since it was based on their own language, and they would understand what was written since it was about their own experiences. But what about a child who does not talk in complete sentences when entering school? What happens when a child cannot dictate a complete sentence? Does the teacher help the child say a complete sentence? What happens to the child who cannot read the sentence back when the teacher writes it because it is not his language? For these children, structured language experience is an important activity.

In her article written over twenty years ago, Pat Cunningham described structured language experience as a writing/reading approach where the majority of children can take part in both the writing and the reading of their "structured language experience sentences." What the children say, the teacher writes; and what the teacher writes, the children can read back later. How is this possible? It is possible if two things happen: the teacher must choose a topic the children know about or are learning about; and the teacher must choose a structure for the children to follow when writing the class sentences (Example: I like to eat _____.). When all the children in the class use the same structure for their dictated sentences, the children who cannot make up sentences on their own can use the chosen pattern and find success. Using the same sentence structure for each sentence on the chart helps all the children in the class take part in the reading/writing experience without having to wait for further language development. Young children learn they can dictate a complete sentence following the chosen sentence pattern. They also learn that they are able to read this same sentence back to the teacher and the class. To be successful, children simply follow the sentence structure used by the children reading the sentences before them.

Some children come to school lacking the skills and understanding that lead to success in beginning reading instruction. Using a predictable chart gives these children a chance to take part in reading and writing instruction with good language models. All children can participate in the instructional activity and get oriented to print at the same time, even if they come from homes where they have not observed adults in reading/writing activities, and they do not know a lot about print and print concepts. Using predictable language (I like..., I see a..., I can..., etc.) makes it easy for all children to say a sentence, see the teacher write the sentence, and then be able to read the sentence back. Because all sentences start the same way, children can remember the sentence and experience success with both the dictation and the subsequent reading of the sentence. After completing several charts, teachers notice that many of the children are ready for something else. That something else is usually "real" writing and reading. Writing predictable charts increases young children's language fluency. Predictable chart activities help young children learn what a sentence is, what a word is, how to talk in complete sentences, and how to track print from left to right and from top to bottom. Cutting apart the sentence helps children who have trouble tracking print understand the concept of a word. Writing predictable charts can lead to a store of basic sight words and gives young children confidence in their abilities to learn to read. Reading begins for all children in the classroom!

Teachers have emergent readers read predictable books so that they can experience success in their early reading. Why not use predictable charts with emergent writers so that they can see that what you say you can write? Once children understand this concept, they can experience success in their early writing. A predictable chart has a predictable pattern (I see..., I like..., My friend is..., etc.). Each sentence on the chart begins the same way. This "predictable" pattern lets all children know what to say when the teacher is writing the chart and, when they are called upon to read the sentences on the chart. Each sentence uses the pattern set up by the teacher and is followed by the name of the child who dictated the sentence in parentheses. For example: My friend is Elaine. (Dottie)

The predictability of these charts and the repetition of the sentences allow all children to experience success. The teacher often says the first sentence and puts her name at the end in parentheses. For the first few sentences, the teacher calls on several students who can complete this task easily. With these sentences as models, almost any child in the class can be called upon to

4

dictate his own sentence. The children know the sentence starter (the "predictable" part of the sentence) and understand how to add their own personal endings. Putting the children's names after the sentences lets the class know which sentences on the chart belong to whom, and lets everyone know that all the children have successfully completed this task.

Month-by-Month Reading and Writing for Kindergarten by Hall and Cunningham suggests introducing predictable charts beginning in October. In one example, after reading the book *Things I Like* by Anthony Browne, the teacher has the children finish the sentence "I like to...." In the November example, the teacher has the children finish the sentence, "I am thankful for...." The book supplies one or two ideas for predictable charts for each month of the school year.

In *The Teacher's Guide to Building Blocks™* by Hall and Williams, predictable charts are an integral part of writing with children in kindergarten. Sample charts and some activities to use with these charts are given for the beginning, middle, and end of the school year. The first charts in the book are simple charts with some simple activities. The later charts are more difficult and include activities that are more developmentally demanding for young children. The first idea for a predictable chart starts with the children's names and can be used very early in the school year. The predictable part of the sentence for this chart is, "My name is...." This chart is easy to make into a class book and can be written very early in the school year with success. "At a Sleepover You Can..." is an example of a predictable chart written after reading the book *Ira Sleeps Over* by Bernard Waber. Young children enjoy telling all the things they can do (or think they can do!) at a sleepover at a relative's or friend's house. One kindergarten child said, "You can stay up late." Another kindergarten student dictated, "You can eat junk food." The answers are as simple or sophisticated as the students you are working with when writing a predictable chart.

This book is devoted entirely to predictable charts; therefore, the subject can be covered in greater depth. We include topics or "chart starters" for 60 charts so that kindergarten and first-grade teachers will have at least one idea for every week of the school year, with some left over. Some of the charts are written to follow the reading of a book or a field trip, or to go along with a theme the class is studying or a special day/time of year. Predictable charts are even more meaningful when they are part of what the teacher is doing and are not done in isolation. After reading *The Little Engine That Could* by Watty Piper, the teacher could write a predictable chart using the starter "I can...." After a field trip to a farm, a fair, or a museum, a popular predictable chart is "I saw a ...." After talking about colors and being introduced to color words, the predictable chart begins, "My favorite color is...." (The teacher writes the sentences with the students' favorite color markers!). After studying about rain in April, the teacher writes a predictable chart about water and the children tell how they use water. For example: We use water to wash our clothes. (Chad). This book will give teachers many ideas for predictable charts from which they can pick and choose as the year progresses.

Introduction

Writing predictable charts helps teachers teach many skills young children need in order to become successful readers and writers. Here are some of the valuable reasons for using predictable charts:

Predictable Charts...

1. **Use the language of the student.**

2. **Enhance the child's self-concept.**

3. **Provide greater opportunity for oral language development.**

4. **Require reading and writing, which are both reinforced by being taught simultaneously.**

5. **Keep reading in its rightful place—interrelated with seeing, hearing, speaking, and writing, and integrated with other curriculum areas.**

6. **Help sound-symbol relationships become meaningful as the teacher goes from the whole (the chart) to the part (a sentence, a word, a letter, or a letter sound).**

7. **Promote divergent thinking as children think of how to finish their sentences.**

8. **Orient the curriculum to both male and female interests.**

9. **Help children become authors as they see their words written down and read by all.**

10. **Foster appreciation for literature when used to follow the reading of a book.**

11. **Help students develop an appreciation and understanding of the <u>abilities</u> of other children in the class.**

12. **Encourage appreciation and understanding for the <u>contributions</u> of other children in the class.**

Five-Day Cycle for Predictable Charts

Ideas for predictable charts come from events and activities that are happening in the classroom. Once a chart is written, the teacher can do a number of activities with the class. These activities contribute to the children's understanding of written language. Usually predictable charts are turned into class big books. These class books are then placed in the "Reading Center" for the children to read and enjoy for the remainder of the year.

Making a class book from a predictable chart is a multilevel activity. By this we mean there is something to be gained by everyone in the class. Some children will be able to read the entire book. Other children can read their own pages and sometimes a few other pages, while also learning a word or two from the structured part of the sentence ("I" and "can" after writing the predictable chart "I Can"). Still other young children are only able to read their own sentences, but they notice that the teacher goes from left to right and top to bottom as she writes the chart. Because the class has dictated the sentences that the teacher has written on the chart and made them into a book, the children know what the book is about. Many children in the class "pretend" read the other pages when they pick up the class big book in the "Reading Center."

Teachers find a five-day cycle works well for each predictable chart made into a big book with the class. Here is what works for most teachers when first attempting this with their classes.

Days 1 and 2: Dictation of the Sentences

First, the teacher reads a book, introduces a topic, or takes the children on a field trip. Next, the teacher gives the students a pattern or model sentence to follow. **The children dictate their sentences using the model given, and the teacher writes the sentences on a large piece of chart paper, putting the children's names in parentheses at the end.** After the dictation of each sentence, the teacher lets the children read their sentences back as she points to the words. Dictation and writing the chart often take one day for a small class and two days if the class is large.

Day 3: Touch Reading the Sentences and Matching Words

On the third day, the teacher asks the students to "touch read" their own sentences on the chart. It helps to move the chart to the students' eye level so they can easily read their sentences and do not have to stretch or crouch down for this task. Using magnets at the top of the chart to hold it on the board makes this possible. **By touching each word on the chart as they read their sentences, the children will learn to "track print."**

Early in the year, the teacher follows the tracking of print by asking the students to count the words in some of the sentences and then the letters in the same sentences. At other times, the teacher has the students find the longest and shortest words in their sentences. The teacher can also discuss capitalization and punctuation.

Once she has made several charts, another activity the teacher can do is to give the children their cut-up sentences in clear, resealable plastic bags. **The teacher calls on two or three of the children to match their cut-up sentences to their written sentences on the predictable chart**. The children place the words in a pocket chart and compare the order of the cut-up words to the order of the words written on the chart. Once the class has seen this modeled by a student (sometimes with the teacher's help), they will all be asked to arrange the words in their cut-up sentences to match their sentences on the predictable chart. While the children are doing this, the teacher walks around the room, monitors the activity, helps the students who need it, and listens to the children read their sentences after matching them to the predictable chart.

Cut-up sentences are an important part of predictable charts. It is hard for some children to track print on a predictable chart even with a pointer. With the cut-up sentences, however, children can see each separate word. Students begin to understand the concept of a word, and they learn that words are separated by spaces in a sentence. Using cut-up sentences, all children can learn what it means to "touch each word" and "track print." Some students also need the experience of matching the order of words in a cut-up sentence to the same sentence written on a predictable chart.

Day 4: Sentence Builders

Today, the teacher focuses on the sentence, each of the words, the sounds of letters, and the letters with an activity called "sentence builders." Before the lesson, the teacher writes three sentences from the chart on sentence strips. She includes the name of the child who dictated the sentence. Next, the teacher cuts the words apart and puts them in an envelope or clear plastic bag, ready to use. The teacher uses one sentence at a time and passes out the words to as many children as she has words, giving the name to the child whose sentence the children are going to build. The students are then asked to be "sentence builders." This means they come to the front of the room, get themselves in the right place in the sentence, and show their words to the class. Some students know their words and can do this task quite easily. Other students have to match the word they are holding to the chart and count words to find their right place. Children often help each other find the right place for each word in the sentence. The child who is holding her name usually knows her correct place is at the end! Finally, the teacher stands behind the sentence builders and touches each child as she reads the words in the sentence with the class. She repeats this process for the other two cut-up sentences.

Once the students are used to "sentence builders," the teacher begins to ask questions about the sentences. Can you find a certain word? Can you find a word that starts like this word? Can you find a word that rhymes with that word? Can you find a word that begins with a certain letter?

9

Introduction

Day 5: Making a Class Book

Begin the lesson by letting the children read their sentences from the chart, one sentence at a time, and then let the class read the chart together with you. After the readings, give each child his cut-up sentence. You will have to prepare these ahead of time! **After you have modeled gluing your sentence on a blank piece of paper, the children put the words in their sentences in the correct order and glue them at the bottoms of sheets of paper. These will serve as the "pages" for the class book**. **Next, the children will illustrate their sentences in the space above the pasted words.** (Early in the year, when many students will have difficulty putting their sentences in order, simply write each child's sentence on the bottom of a blank sheet of paper.)

The teacher makes a book cover and staples or binds the pages together. Now the students have a class big book to treasure all year! As the year progresses and the class makes more class books, the teacher gives the sentence strips to the students and lets the students cut the words in their sentences apart. She may also mix up the words in the sentences so the students have to paste them in the right order, as well as cut the words apart. This is an important step for those children who can cut and paste the words when they are given in the correct order but now are asked to do a more complex step—cutting, reordering, and pasting words in the correct order on the piece of paper. Another more challenging task for the children on day five is to let them copy or type their sentences for the book. The more the children learn, the more work you can give them to do!

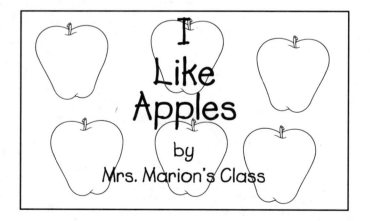

Examples of Easy (Early) Predictable Charts

One of the easiest charts to begin with is, "My name is...." (Since teachers usually start the year doing some get acquainted activities to learn the students' names, this is not only an easy chart, but a useful one as well.) The teacher writes "Names" on the top of the chart. The first sentence she may write is "My name is Mrs. Hall." Then, the teacher calls on the students to dictate their sentences, and she writes what the children say ("My name is <u>Joey</u>."). One by one, each child uses the model provided and completes the sentence with his name. On the fifth and final day, each child gets a sheet of paper on which the teacher has written, "My name is" and each student writes his own name and draws his picture on the page. The finished product is a class book!

Another popular easy chart for the beginning of the school year is about colors. The children spend a few days at the beginning of the school year talking about each of the colors and the color words. When the class has completed the eight "basic" colors, the teacher gives the children circles cut from their favorite colors of paper. Then, they write their names on the color circles. Together, the teacher and the class graph their favorite colors using these circles of paper by pasting them under each color word on a large sheet of bulletin board paper. The finished graph looks like this:

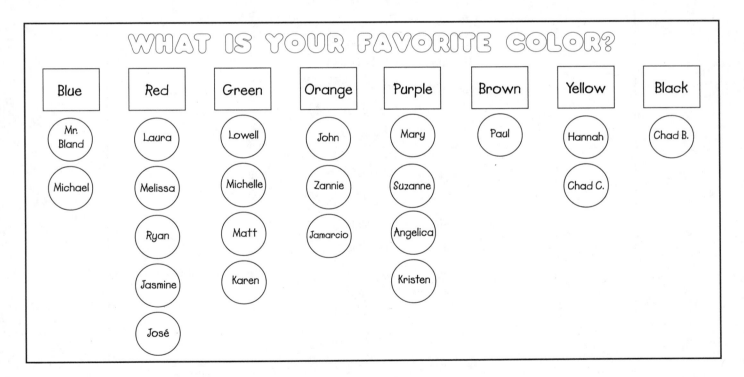

This graph helps each child to say or dictate a sentence about his favorite color, "My favorite color is..." or even easier, "I like...." Each child finishes the predictable sentence with her color, and the teacher repeats the words and writes the sentence on a large piece of lined chart paper using that child's favorite color of marker.

Introduction

The finished chart looks like this:

```
                              Colors
                      I like blue. (Mr. Bland)
        (The above sentence is written with a thick, blue marker.)
                        I like red. (Laura)
        (The above sentence is written with a thick, red marker.)
                      I like green. (Lowell)
        (The above sentence is written with a thick, green marker.)
                      I like orange. (John)
        (The above sentence is written with a thick, orange marker.)
                      I like purple. (Mary)
        (The above sentence is written with a thick, purple marker.)
                      I like brown. (Paul)
        (The above sentence is written with a thick, brown marker.)
                     I like yellow. (Hannah)
        (The above sentence is written with a thick, yellow marker.)
                      I like red. (Melissa)
                      I like blue. (Michael)
                     I like green. (Michelle)
                     I like purple. (Suzanne)
                       I like red. (Ryan)
                     I like yellow. (Chad C.)
                     I like black. (Chad B.)
                     I like orange. (Zannie)
                      I like green. (Matt)
                     I like red. (Jasmine)
                    I like orange. (Jamarcio)
                      I like red. (José)
                    I like purple. (Angelica)
                    I like purple. (Kristen)
                     I like green. (Karen)
```

Days 1 and 2: Dictation and Writing of the Sentences

The teacher talks about all the colors, reviewing what the class has learned for the past week or two. Each child writes his name with his favorite color of marker or crayon and draws a picture using that color. The teacher helps the students graph their favorite colors on the first day, and they begin the dictation of their sentences ("I like...."). The children dictate their predictable sentences as the teacher writes them on a large piece of chart paper. The dictation and the writing of the predictable chart is completed on the second day. The teacher begins the predictable chart with her sentence, "I like blue. (Mrs. Hall)," making sure to put her name in parentheses after the sentence. When the teacher writes the sentence, she is modeling for the children what they will do next. The teacher keeps this in mind when choosing the children to dictate the sentences. She starts with students who can do the task easily so that those students who may have more diffi-culty can hear several examples. (Early in the year, the selection of the first few students is critical; the first children chosen should be students who find the task easy.)

Day 3: Touch Reading the Sentences

On the third day, the teacher asks each of the students to "touch read" his sentence on the chart. Each child reads his sentence, "I like . . . ," filling in the blank with his favorite color. The color of the print is another clue for these young students. If you have chosen wisely, the first few children can "touch read" successfully and will be models for those who need to watch several children before they feel confident. Remember, cut-up sentences will help some children learn this task.

Day 4: Sentence Builders

On the fourth day, the teacher focuses on the sentence, the words, the sounds of letters, and the letters. Before the lesson, the teacher writes three sentences from the chart on three separate sentence strips. The name of the child who dictated the sentence is included at the end of the sentence. The teacher cuts the words apart and puts them in an envelope or a resealable plastic bag, ready for use. The teacher uses one sentence at a time and passes out the words in that sentence to four children. She makes sure to give the name to the child whose sentence she is going to build. The teacher sometimes chooses a sentence because a child needs a self-esteem booster, and she knows the child can read his own name and do this task correctly. These four students are then asked to be "sentence builders." To do this activity, the child holding "I" has to get at the beginning of the sentence. The next place in line belongs to the child holding "like." In the third place is the child holding the color word. In the fourth place is the child holding his name. Finally, the teacher stands behind the "sentence builders" and touches each child as she reads the sentence with the class. The teacher repeats this process for the other two cut-up sentences.

Day 5: Making a Class Book

Some teachers write the first few sentences from the predictable chart on the bottom of large pieces of drawing paper for the children to illustrate. If this is at the beginning of the school year and one of the first predictable charts your class is making into a book, this is one option available to make the task easier. For the *Colors* class book, all the children have to do to illustrate their sentences is to draw something in the color they like. To finish the book, the teacher makes a front cover, including the title, and a plain back cover. Finally, she staples the pages inside in the order they appear on the chart. Now the students have a class big book with all the names of the students in their class inside. It is a big book many of them can read because the names of their classmates are "interesting to them."

Introduction

Other easy predictable "I" charts to make early in the school year (See pages 21-30):

I can . . .	I am . . .
I like to . . .	I will . . .
I do not like to . . .	I went . . .
I have a . . .	I will go . . .
I see . . .	I like to eat . . .

Activities to Make Predictable Charts More Challenging

Many teachers claim that some of their students find these tasks become "easy." Often, these teachers abandon predictable charts and the associated activities before *all* children reach their potential. Clever teachers keep doing these activities, but make them more challenging and appealing to their students as they grow and learn. Here are some clever "twists" and additions to the five-day cycle of activities for predictable charts.

Predictable Charts Following Books

As a part of a kindergarten or first-grade theme on animals, a teacher could read *A Is for Animals* by David Pelham. After the teacher reads this alphabet book, students dictate sentences which the teacher writes on the predictable chart, "A Is for Animals." The children supply the names of the animals for each letter of the alphabet. For this chart, the letter sequence is the predictable part of the sentences. This is how the chart would appear:

A Is for Animals	
A is for antelope. (Mr. Bland)	N is for night crawler. (Hannah)
B is for bear. (Chad C.)	O is for octopus. (Jamarcio)
C is for cat. (Suzanne)	P is for panda. (Angelica)
D is for dog. (Ryan)	Q is for quail. (Jasmine)
E is for elephant. (Michelle)	R is for rabbit. (Zannie)
F is for fish. (Chad B.)	S is for seal. (Melissa)
G is for goat. (Michael)	T is for tiger. (José)
H is for horse. (Hannah)	U is for unicorn. (Kristen)
I is for iguana. (Laura)	V is for vulture. (Karen)
J is for joey. (John)	W is for walrus. (Melissa)
K is for kangaroo. (Paul)	X is for ox. (Matthew)
L is for llama. (Lowell)	Y is for yak. (Hannah)
M is for mouse. (Mary)	Z is for zebra. (Chad C.)

Days 1 and 2: Dictation of the Sentences

The teacher reads the alphabet book and talks about animals and letters with his class. "Does anyone know an animal whose name begins with an 'a'? With a 'b'?" For the "easy" letters like **b** (bear), **c** (cat), **d** (dog), **t** (tiger), etc., the teacher calls on the children who may find this activity difficult. He saves the harder letters like **i**, **o**, and **x**, to do together with the class, or he just uses the animal names in the book. (If you do not have 26 children, plan this so that you or the book are supplying the harder letters for this task.) It will take two days to do sentence dictation and write the predictable chart for the 26 letters of the alphabet. A teacher who has a small number of students (How lucky!) can read, discuss, and begin dictation on the first day, then have some children dictate another sentence on the second day. To make the activity even more challenging, read *Animalia* by Graeme Base, and write tongue twisters for each letter of the alphabet!

Day 3: Touch Reading the Sentences and Matching

On the third day, the teacher asks each student to "touch read" her own sentence on the chart. Each child reads, "____ is for ____," supplying both the letter name and the animal name for her sentence, as well as reading her name at the end. The teacher and the class start at the top of the chart and read to the bottom, with each child taking a turn. When the "touch reading" is finished, the teacher may ask for the biggest (longest) animal name or the smallest (shortest). He may ask the students to clap the sounds they hear in the different animal names. For example, **an-te-lope** (3 claps), **bear** (1 clap), **el-e-phant** (3 claps), **hip-po-pot-a-mus** (5 claps!), **ze-bra** (2 claps), etc.

Day 4: Sentence Builders

Today, the teacher focuses on the sentence, the words, the sounds of letters, and the letters. Before the lesson, the teacher writes three sentences from the chart on three sentence strips, including the names of the children who dictated the sentences. She cuts apart the words for each sentence and puts them in an envelope or a resealable plastic bag, ready to use in class. The teacher uses one sentence at a time and passes out the words to some children, making sure to give the name to the child whose sentence they are going to build. The students are then asked to be "sentence builders" and stand with their word cards in the right sequence. Finally, the teacher stands behind the "sentence builders," touching the children as she reads their sentence with the class. The teacher repeats this process for the other two cut-up sentences.

Day 5: Making a Class Book

Each child each gets her own sentence. The words for the sentences are cut apart. Now the children have to put the words in their sentences in the correct sequence. The teacher checks the children's sentences, then instructs them to glue the words, in order, along the bottoms of their book pages. When the sentences are correctly glued at the bottoms of their pages, the children illustrate their sentences by drawing pictures of their animals on their pages. To finish the book, the teacher makes a front cover, including the title *A Is for Animals*, and a plain back cover. He staples the pages inside in the order they appear on the chart. Now the students have another class book to put in the Reading Center!

Introduction

Predictable Charts Following Field Trips

Depending upon where you live, during the late summer or fall is fair time. It is time to see the best of the animals, vegetables, flowers, and home cooking, as well as ride the rides and eat "fair food." Teachers of young children find this to be a valuable field trip. The weeks before and after the trip to the fair are filled with class discussions of the animals, foods, and sights that are all part of the experience. Following the trip to the fair, the teacher begins a predictable chart about what the students saw at the fair. He titles the chart, "At the Fair" and he begins each sentence with, "I saw a...." The children dictate to him what they saw. After the children have dictated their sentences, the completed chart might look like this:

At the Fair	
I saw rides. (Mr. Bland)	I saw a big pumpkin. (Jamarcio)
I saw animals. (Paul)	I saw chickens. (Angelica)
I saw baby cows. (Hannah)	I saw cows. (José)
I saw apples. (Mary)	I saw an elephant. (Chad C.)
I saw horses. (John)	I saw a big slide. (Chad B.)
I saw goats. (Lowell)	I saw a merry-go-round. (Kristen)
I saw sheep. (Laura)	I saw cakes and pies. (Karen)
I saw food. (Melissa)	I saw lots of people. (Matthew)
I saw ponies. (Ryan)	I saw some pigs. (Zannie)
I saw candy apples. (Suzanne)	I saw some corn. (Jasmine)
I saw games. (Michelle)	

Days 1 and 2: Dictation and Writing the Sentences

Day one is the trip to the fair. On the next day, the teacher discusses the fair with the class. They discuss what they saw, what they did, and what they could not do (sometimes the rides are not operating and the games are not open). They talk about the animals. "Did any animals have ribbons?" Next, they discuss the exhibits for the biggest pumpkin, the most creative pumpkin decoration, the best apple pie, and the children's artwork. After the discussion, the dictation and writing of the predictable chart begin. The chart is finished on the second day.

Day 3: Touch Reading the Sentences and Matching

On the third day, the teacher asks each student to "touch read" his own sentence on the chart. The teacher lets the children finger point to the words in their sentences as they read them. This is an easy task for the sentence, "I saw goats." Early in the year, it is a harder task when a sentence has the word "pumpkin" or "elephant" in it. Young children want to point to a word for each sound they hear. They get confused until they realize that "big" words have lots of letters and more than one sound. The teacher and the class start reading at the top of the chart and read to the bottom. Each child takes a turn reading his own sentence. Children that need a little extra help are not called on for a sentence at the beginning of the chart. Instead, the teacher waits until near the end of the activity so that these students have a chance to hear others read.

After "touch reading," the students take their cut-up sentences (which the teacher or assistant has prepared ahead of time), go back to their desks, and match the words in their cut-up sentences to the words on the chart. By using the sentences on the predictable chart as a model, most children can do this task. The teacher's job is to circulate, help when needed, and show the children how to use the chart to self-check and self-correct. He will also listen as the children read the sentences they have built on their desks.

Day 4: Sentence Builders

Today, the teacher focuses on the sentence, the words, the sounds of letters, and the letters. Before the lesson, the teacher writes three sentences from the chart on three sentence strips. The names of the children who dictated the sentences are included at the end of these sentences. He cuts apart the words and puts them in an envelope or plastic bag, ready to use in class. The teacher uses one sentence at a time and passes out the words to some children, making sure to give the name to the child whose sentence he is going to build. The students are asked to be "sentence builders" and arrange themselves in the correct order, using the chart for guidance as necessary. Finally, the teacher stands behind the "sentence builders" and touches each child as he reads their "built" sentence with the class. The teacher repeats this process for the other two cut-up sentences.

Day 5: Making a Class Book

Today, each child gets a resealable plastic bag with her own sentence in it. The words in each sentence are cut apart. Next, the children have to put the words in the correct order and glue them at the bottoms of their papers. Then, the children have to illustrate the sentences on their pages. The teacher decides that for this book, he will put everything in sequence. He will list all 23 things at the fair according to what they saw first, second, third, etc. This takes a little longer but also teaches another valuable skill. To finish the book, the teacher makes a front cover, including the title *Our Trip to the Fair*, and a plain back cover. Finally, he staples the pages inside. Now the students have added another class book to the Reading Center!

Predictable Charts for Topics or Themes

Spring is the time of year when people plant, no matter where they live. Some areas plant earlier in the season, while other areas plant later. "Plants" is a popular theme during April or May. Many teachers talk about plants and how they grow. Some kindergarten classes plant carrot, bean, or marigold seeds. The children are amazed to see a little seed sprout into a plant right before their eyes in the classroom. They learn how to plant seeds and that plants need soil, water, and sunshine to grow.

Introduction

Here is a predictable chart one teacher came up with for plants:

In My Garden	
I will plant watermelon. (Mr. Bland)	I will plant geraniums. (Chad B.)
I will plant carrots. (Chad C.)	I will plant zucchini. (Michelle)
I will plant onions. (Lowell)	I will plant strawberries. (José)
I will plant tomatoes. (Ryan)	I will plant roses. (John)
I will plant flowers. (Suzanne)	I will plant cantaloupe. (Paul)
I will plant azaleas. (Laura)	I will plant tomatoes. (Michael)
I will plant tulips. (Melissa)	I will plant beans. (Matthew)
I will plant lilies. (Mary)	I will plant flowers. (Jasmine)
I will plant green beans. (Jamarcio)	I will plant tulips. (Karen)
I will plant radishes. (Angelica)	I will plant all kinds of vegetables. (Kristen)
I will plant marigolds. (Hannah)	

Days 1 and 2: Dictation and Writing the Sentences

Many teachers use a few weeks in April or May to help children learn about plants. They may even plant a garden or individual seed cups. The teacher begins the sentence dictation and writing of the chart on the first day of the week and finishes this task on the second day. Each child tells the teacher something that they would like to plant in the garden and completes this predictable sentence starter, "I will plant...."

Day 3: Touch Reading the Sentences and Matching

On the third day, the teacher asks each student to "touch read" her own sentence on the chart. The teacher lets each child finger point to each word in her sentence as she reads it. By this time of the year, "touch reading" is an easy task for many of the students, so the teacher will use the cut-up sentences for tomorrow's lesson to do some "matching" today. The children use their sentences from the predictable chart as their models. The teacher circulates, helps when needed, and listens to the children as they read their sentences.

Day 4: Sentence Builders

Today, the teacher focuses on the sentence, the words, the sounds of the letters, and the letters themselves. Before the lesson, the teacher chooses three sentences from the chart that the students used for matching words the day before; these sentences will be used today for sentence builders. The teacher uses one sentence at a time and passes out the words to some children, making sure to give the name to the child whose sentence the class is going to build. The students are then asked to become "sentence builders." The students arrange themselves in the correct order, using the chart for guidance as necessary. Finally, the teacher stands behind the "sentence

18

builders" and touches each child as he reads their "built" sentence with the class. The teacher repeats this process for the other two cut-up sentences.

Day 5: Making a Class Book

The children each get their own cut-up sentence from the predictable chart. Next, the children have to put their words in the correct order and glue the words at the bottoms of their papers. The children then illustrate their pages. To finish the book, the teacher makes a front cover, including the title *In My Garden*, and a plain back cover. Finally, he staples the pages inside in the order they appear on the chart. Once again, the students have added a class-made book to the Reading Center!

How Writing a Predictable Chart Is a Multilevel Activity

Predictable charts are dictated by the children and written by the teacher. They are multilevel because children can learn many things, depending upon their level of literacy development. When children are writing a predictable sentence with the teacher, some children are learning that what they say they can write, while others are learning to read what the teacher has written. Some children are learning that we write from left to right, and we start at the top of the page and work to the bottom. Still other kindergarten students may even be learning how to punctuate sentences. While some children are learning how to read all the words, others may be learning how to write all the words. When the students dictate words to the teacher, see the teacher write these words down on paper, and then hear her read them back to the class, all children learn more about reading and writing. What they learn depends upon what they already know and where they are in their literacy learning. Completing predictable charts is just one example of writing *with* children, but it is a very important one. Predictable charts provide another opportunity for all kindergarten and first-grade students to see themselves as readers and writers.

Using Predictable Charts Can:

- increase exposure to print and book awareness
- make stories more meaningful to children
- illustrate the left to right print concept
- illustrate top to bottom directionality
- help students see that words are units
- help students see that words are separated by spaces
- promote sound awareness
- encourage students to notice likenesses and differences
- facilitate learning about the alphabet
- promote learning about writing
- help students see the natural flow of language

Introduction

- give students exposure to writing and reading skills
- promote individual reading success
- develop word and sight recognition
- develop "one word/one touch" awareness through finger pointing
- develop awareness that print conveys meaning
- develop awareness that thoughts are expressed in complex sentences
- develop better word recognition
- develop awareness of uppercase and lowercase letters
- encourage students to contribute to class stories
- encourage students to respond to printed materials
- help students recall experiences
- teach children to read dictated stories
- give students the opportunity to develop an understanding of a class story

Predictable charts are part of the Building Blocks™ framework for reading and writing in kindergarten. All students need the experiences that writing and reading predictable charts provide. They help all children experience success in writing and reading, regardless of their entering literacy levels. They help children understand the jargon of school. They help students learn that our English language is made up of sentences, and sentences have words in them. Predictable charts help children see that words are made up of letters, and letter have sounds associated with them. There are so many wonderful things for children to learn about reading, writing, and the world of print; predictable charts provide a way for young students to learn these things more easily.

I Can

Some typical responses:

> I Can
> I can sing. (Mrs. Russell)
> I can read. (Pat)
> I can draw. (David)
> I can write. (Jim)
> I can count. (Joyce)

Materials:

- lined chart paper (preferably manila tagboard)
- magic markers
- white or manila construction paper (usually 12" x 18")
- sentence strips, scissors, glue
- crayons

Procedure:

- The teacher talks about the things children in the class can do.
- Children dictate their sentences as the teacher writes them on a chart.
- Each child "touch reads" her own sentence on the chart.
- "Sentence builders" focuses on sentences, words, letters, and letter-sounds.
- Sentences on sentence strips are cut apart, glued on construction paper, then illustrated by students to make the pages of a class book.

Things I Like To Do

Some typical responses:

> Things I Like To Do
> I like to read. (Ms. Brown)
> I like to e-mail. (Ryan)
> I like to color. (Suzanne)
> I like to plant. (Chad)
> I like to ride in the car. (Michael)

Materials:

- lined chart paper (preferably manila tagboard)
- magic markers
- white or manila construction paper (usually 12" x 18")
- sentence strips, scissors, glue
- crayons

Procedure:

- The teacher talks about the things the children in the class like to do.
- Children dictate their sentences as the teacher writes them on a chart.
- Each child "touch reads" his own sentence on the chart.
- "Sentence builders" focuses on sentences, words, letters, and letter-sounds.
- Sentences on sentence strips are cut apart, glued on construction paper, then illustrated by students to make the pages of a class book.

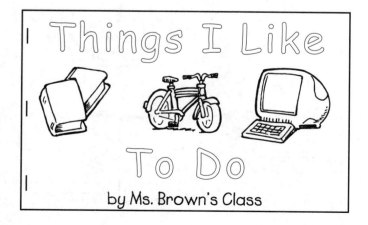

Things I Do Not Like To Do

Some typical responses:

> Things I Do Not Like To Do
> I do not like to clean up. (Mr. Robson)
> I do not like to sing. (Laura)
> I do not like to wait in line. (Diane)
> I do not like to play football. (Angie)
> I do not like to play t-ball. (Joe)

Materials:

- lined chart paper (preferably manila tagboard)
- magic markers
- white or manila construction paper (usually 12" x 18")
- sentence strips, scissors, glue
- crayons

Procedure:

- The teacher talks about the things the children in the class do not like to do.
- Children dictate their sentences as the teacher writes them on a chart.
- Each child "touch reads" his own sentence on the chart.
- "Sentence builders" focuses on sentences, words, letters, and letter-sounds.
- Sentences on sentence strips are cut apart, glued on construction paper, then illustrated by students to make the pages of a class book. book.

Things I Have

Some typical responses:

> Things I Have
> I have a cat. (Mrs. Hunnicutt)
> I have a computer. (Ryan)
> I have a dog. (Jerry)
> I have a airplane. (Craig)
> I have a doll. (DyAnn)

Materials:

- lined chart paper (preferably manila tagboard)
- magic markers
- white or manila construction paper (usually 12" x 18")
- sentence strips, scissors, glue
- crayons

Procedure:

- The teacher talks about the things the children in the class have.
- Children dictate their sentences as the teacher writes them on a chart.
- Each child "touch reads" his own sentence on the chart.
- "Sentence builders" focuses on sentences, words, letters, and letter-sounds.
- Sentences on sentence strips are cut apart, glued on construction paper, then illustrated by students to make the pages of a class book.

I have a dog. (Jerry)

I See

Some typical responses:

> I See
> I see the alphabet. (Mrs. Hall)
> I see books. (Richard)
> I see centers. (Judy)
> I see desks. (Gladys)
> I see color words. (Bob)

Materials:

- lined chart paper (preferably manila tagboard)
- magic markers
- white or manila construction paper (usually 12" x 18")
- sentence strips, scissors, glue
- crayons

Procedure:

- The teacher talks about the things the children in the class see in the classroom.
- Children dictate their sentences as the teacher writes them on a chart.
- Each child "touch reads" her own sentence on the chart.
- "Sentence builders" focuses on sentences, words, letters, and letter-sounds.
- Sentences on sentence strips are cut apart, glued on construction paper, then illustrated by students to make the pages of a class book.

Me

Some typical responses:

> Me
> I am a teacher. (Mrs. Ashby)
> I am a boy. (Mark)
> I am smart. (Laura)
> I am five. (Ben)
> I am strong. (Lonnie)

Materials:

- lined chart paper (preferably manila tagboard)
- magic markers
- white or manila construction paper (usually 12" x 18")
- sentence strips, scissors, glue
- crayons

Procedure:

- The teacher begins the discussion with, "I am a teacher." and then talks about the things children can say: "I am five," "I am a girl," "I am good in school," etc.
- Children dictate their sentences as the teacher writes them on a chart.
- Each child "touch reads" his own sentence on the chart.
- "Sentence builders" focuses on sentences, words, letters, and letter-sounds.
- Sentences on sentence strips are cut apart, glued on construction paper, then illustrated by students to make the pages of a class book.

Me
by Mrs. Ashby's Class
I am five.   I am a girl.

I am strong. (Lonnie)

Today I Will

Some typical responses:

> Today I Will
> I will read. (Miss Simon)
> I will listen. (Kelly)
> I will draw. (Andy)
> I will run. (Kim)
> I will play outside. (Drew)

Materials:

- lined chart paper (preferably manila tagboard)
- magic markers
- white or manila construction paper (usually 12" x 18")
- sentence strips, scissors, glue
- crayons

Procedure:

- The teacher talks about the many things the children in the class will do today.
- Children dictate their sentences as the teacher writes them on a chart.
- Each child "touch reads" her own sentence on the chart.
- "Sentence builders" focuses on sentences, words, letters, and letter-sounds.
- Sentences on sentence strips are cut apart, glued on construction paper, then illustrated by students to make the pages of a class book.

Today I Will
by Miss Simon's Class

I will run. (Kim)

For the Break

Some typical responses:

> For the Break
> I will go to Disneyland. (Mrs. Gingras)
> I will go to the mountains. (Karen)
> I will go to the lake. (Matthew)
> I will go hiking. (Suzanne)
> I will go to the beach. (Kristen)

*Disneyland is a registered trademark of Disney Enterprises, Inc.

Materials:

- lined chart paper (preferably manila tagboard)
- magic markers
- white or manila construction paper (usually 12" x 18")
- sentence strips, scissors, glue
- crayons

Procedure:

- The teacher talks about the places the children in the class can visit.
- Children dictate their sentences as the teacher writes them on a chart.
- Each child "touch reads" his own sentence on the chart.
- "Sentence builders" focuses on sentences, words, letters, and letter-sounds.
- Sentences on sentence strips are cut apart, glued on construction paper, then illustrated by students to make the pages of a class book.

Over the Break

Some typical responses:

> Over the Break
> I went to my friend's house. (Mrs. Murphy)
> I went to my aunt's house. (Zannie)
> I went to the beach. (Joe)
> I went fishing. (Johnny)
> I went to the desert. (Marc)

Materials:

- lined chart paper (preferably manila tagboard)
- magic markers
- white or manila construction paper (usually 12" x 18")
- sentence strips, scissors, glue
- crayons

Procedure:

- The teacher talks about the places the children went while they were off from school.
- Children dictate their sentences as the teacher writes them on a chart.
- Each child "touch reads" her own sentence on the chart.
- "Sentence builders" focuses on sentences, words, letters, and letter-sounds.
- Sentences on sentence strips are cut apart, glued on construction paper, then illustrated by students to make the pages of a class book.

Food

Some typical responses:

> **Food**
> I like to eat pizza. (Mrs. Costello)
> I like to eat macaroni. (Kathy)
> I like to eat clams. (Ray)
> I like to eat bread. (Jeanne)
> I like to eat fish. (Stuart)

Materials:

- lined chart paper (preferably manila tagboard)
- magic markers
- white or manila construction paper (usually 12" x 18")
- sentence strips, scissors, glue
- crayons

Procedure:

- The teacher talks about the things the children in the class like to eat.
- Children dictate their sentences as the teacher writes them on a chart.
- Each child "touch reads" his own sentence on the chart.
- "Sentence builders" focuses on sentences, words, letters, and letter-sounds.
- Sentences on sentence strips are cut apart, glued on construction paper, then illustrated by students to make the pages of a class book.

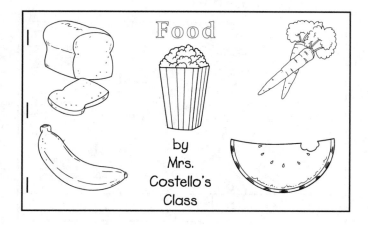

Food
by
Mrs.
Costello's
Class

I like to eat fish. (Stuart)

The Little Engine That Could
by Watty Piper (Grosett & Dunlap, 1978)

Some typical responses:

> I Can
> I can write. (Mrs. Boger)
> I can draw. (Angela)
> I can brush my teeth. (Allie)
> I can ride my bike. (Alex)
> I can jump rope. (Amie)

Materials:

- lined chart paper (preferably manila tagboard)
- magic markers
- white or manila construction paper (usually 12" x 18")
- sentence strips, scissors, glue
- crayons

Procedure:

- The teacher talks about the things children in the class can do by themselves.
- Children dictate their sentences as the teacher writes them on a chart.
- Each child "touch reads" his own sentence on the chart.
- "Sentence builders" focuses on sentences, words, letters, and letter-sounds.
- Sentences on sentence strips are cut apart, glued on construction paper, then illustrated by students to make the pages of a class book.

Things I Like
by Anthony Browne (Houghton Mifflin Co., 1994)

Some typical responses:

> Things I Like
> I like to walk. (Mrs. Fansler)
> I like to run. (Wesley)
> I like to read. (Marie)
> I like to make puzzles. (Andrew)
> I like to ride my bike. (Kim)

Materials:

- lined chart paper (preferably manila tagboard)
- magic markers
- white or manila construction paper (usually 12" x 18")
- sentence strips, scissors, glue
- crayons

Procedure:

- The teacher talks about the things children in the class like.
- Children dictate their sentences as the teacher writes them on a chart.
- Each child "touch reads" his own sentence on the chart.
- "Sentence builders" focuses on sentences, words, letters, and letter-sounds.
- Sentences on sentence strips are cut apart, glued on construction paper, then illustrated by students to make the pages of a class book.

My Head Is Full of Colors
by Catherine Friend (Hyperion Books, 1994)

Some typical responses:

> My Head Is Full of...
> My head is full of books. (Ms. Corkrean)
> My head is full of cats. (Shawn)
> My head is full of friends. (Michelle)
> My head is full of flowers. (Stanley)
> My head is full of food. (Chad)

Materials:

- lined chart paper (preferably manila tagboard)
- magic markers
- white or manila construction paper (usually 12" x 18")
- sentence strips, scissors, glue
- crayons

Procedure:

- The teacher talks about the things children in the class think about.
- Children dictate their sentences as the teacher writes them on a chart.
- Each child "touch reads" her own sentence on the chart.
- "Sentence builders" focuses on sentences, words, letters, and letter-sounds.
- Sentences on sentence strips are cut apart, glued on construction paper, then illustrated by students to make the pages of a class book.

33

Green Eggs and Ham

by Dr. Seuss (Random House, 1976)

Some typical responses:

> I Don't Like...
> I don't like green eggs. (Mrs. Hunnicutt)
> I don't like cheese. (Ryan)
> I don't like fish. (Jerry)
> I don't like onions. (Craig)
> I don't like liver. (DyAnn)

Materials:

- lined chart paper (preferably manila tagboard)
- magic markers
- white or manila construction paper (usually 12" x 18")
- sentence strips, scissors, glue
- crayons

Procedure:

- The teacher talks about the things children in the class do *not* like.
- Children dictate their sentences as the teacher writes them on a chart.
- Each child "touch reads" her own sentence on the chart.
- "Sentence builders" focuses on sentences, words, letters, and letter-sounds.
- Sentences on sentence strips are cut apart, glued on construction paper, then illustrated by students to make the pages of a class book.

*Eating the Alphabet**

by Lois Ehlert (Voyager Books, 1989)

Some typical responses:

> Food Alphabet
> A is for apple. (Mr. Bland)
> B is for bananas. (Tracy)
> C is for carrots. (Steve)
> D is for drinks. (Janet)
> E is for eggs. (Patti)

*A predictable alphabet chart can be completed after reading any alphabet book.

Materials:

- lined chart paper (preferably manila tagboard)
- magic markers
- white or manila construction paper (usually 12" x 18")
- sentence strips, scissors, glue
- crayons

Procedure:

- The teacher talks about the different foods the children like to eat.
- Children dictate their sentences as the teacher writes them on a chart.
- Each child "touch reads" his own sentence on the chart.
- "Sentence builders" focuses on sentences, words, letters, and letter-sounds.
- Sentences on sentence strips are cut apart, glued on construction paper, then illustrated by students to make the pages of a class book.

The Relatives Came
by Cynthia Rylant (Aladdin Books, 1985)

Some typical responses:

> ### My Relatives
> My relatives like to eat. (Mrs. Ayers)
> My relatives like to shop. (Mark)
> My relatives like to race cars. (Laura)
> My relatives like to read. (Ben)
> My relatives like to talk. (Lonnie)

Materials:

- lined chart paper (preferably manila tagboard)
- magic markers
- white or manila construction paper (usually 12" x 18")
- sentence strips, scissors, glue
- crayons

Procedure:

- The teacher talks about the children's relatives and what they do with their relatives.
- Children dictate their sentences as the teacher writes them on a chart.
- Each child "touch reads" his own sentence on the chart.
- "Sentence builders" focuses on sentences, words, letters, and letter-sounds.
- Sentences on sentence strips are cut apart, glued on construction paper, then illustrated by students to make the pages of a class book.

> # My Relatives
> by
> Mrs. Ayers's Class

My relatives like to talk. (Lonnie)

Johnny Appleseed
by Steven Kellogg (Scholastic, Inc., 1985)

Some typical responses:

> I Like Apples
> I like red apples. (Miss Marion)
> I like yellow apples. (Susie)
> I like green apples. (Kristen)
> I like red apples. (Roger)
> I like green apples. (Ben)

Materials:

- lined chart paper (preferably manila tagboard)
- magic markers
- white or manila construction paper (usually 12" x 18")
- sentence strips, scissors, glue
- crayons

Procedure:

- The teacher talks about Johnny Appleseed and all the different types of apples.
- Children dictate their sentences as the teacher writes them on a chart.
- Each child "touch reads" her own sentence on the chart.
- "Sentence builders" focuses on sentences, words, letters, and letter-sounds.
- Sentences on sentence strips are cut apart, glued on construction paper, then illustrated by students to make the pages of a class book.

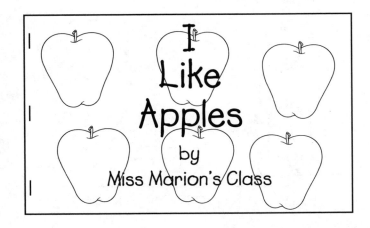

Dear Santa
by Alan Benjamin (Simon & Schuster, 1993)

Some typical responses:

> For the Holidays I Want...
> I want a sled. (Mrs. Reckord)
> I want a bike. (Jackson)
> I want a boat. (Gary)
> I want a doll. (Heidi)
> I want a scooter. (Haiden)

Materials:

- lined chart paper (preferably manila tagboard)
- magic markers
- white or manila construction paper (usually 12" x 18")
- sentence strips, scissors, glue
- crayons

Procedure:

- The teacher talks about the things the children want for holiday gifts.
- Children dictate their sentences as the teacher writes them on a chart.
- Each child "touch reads" her own sentence on the chart.
- "Sentence builders" focuses on sentences, words, letters, and letter-sounds.
- Sentences on sentence strips are cut apart, glued on construction paper, then illustrated by students to make the pages of a class book.

In a People House
by Dr. Seuss (Random House, 1973)

Some typical responses:

> In a People House
> You see chairs. (Mrs. Greene)
> You see beds. (Glenda)
> You see pictures. (Rusty)
> You see dishes. (Katherine)
> You see towels. (Gray)

Materials:

- lined chart paper (preferably manila tagboard)
- magic markers
- white or manila construction paper (usually 12" x 18")
- sentence strips, scissors, glue
- crayons

Procedure:

- The teacher talks about the things the children see in their houses.
- Children dictate their sentences as the teacher writes them on a chart.
- Each child "touch reads" his own sentence on the chart.
- "Sentence builders" focuses on sentences, words, letters, and letter-sounds.
- Sentences on sentence strips are cut apart, glued on construction paper, then illustrated by students to make the pages of a class book.

39

Arthur Writes a Story*

by Marc Brown (Little, Brown & Co., 1998)

Some typical responses:

> Arthur
> Arthur likes pets. (Mrs. Wigley)
> Arthur likes computers. (Seth)
> Arthur likes basketball. (Steve)
> Arthur likes to play. (Olivia)
> Arthur likes to write stories. (Linda)

*Any *Arthur* book by Marc Brown will work for this chart.

Materials:

- lined chart paper (preferably manila tagboard)
- magic markers
- white or manila construction paper (usually 12" x 18")
- sentence strips, scissors, glue
- crayons

Procedure:

- The teacher talks about the things that Arthur does in this book and on TV.
- Children dictate their sentences as the teacher writes them on a chart.
- Each child "touch reads" his own sentence on the chart.
- "Sentence builders" focuses on sentences, words, letters, and letter-sounds.
- Sentences on sentence strips are cut apart, glued on construction paper, then illustrated by students to make the pages of a class book.

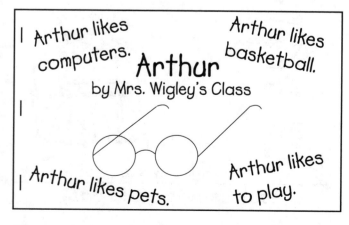

At the Zoo

Some typical responses:

> At the Zoo
> I saw animals. (Mrs. Leonard)
> I saw a tiger. (Randy)
> I saw a bear. (Helene)
> I saw a zebra. (Ginger)
> I saw a monkey. (Janet)

Materials:

- lined chart paper (preferably manila tagboard)
- magic markers
- white or manila construction paper (usually 12" x 18")
- sentence strips, scissors, glue
- crayons

Procedure:

- The teacher talks about all the things the class saw at the zoo.
- Children dictate their sentences as the teacher writes them on a chart.
- Each child "touch reads" her own sentence on the chart.
- "Sentence builders" focuses on sentences, words, letters, and letter-sounds.
- Sentences on sentence strips are cut apart; glued on construction paper, then illustrated by students to make the pages of a class book.

At the Farm

Some typical responses:

> At the Farm
> I saw cows. (Mrs. Harper)
> I saw goats. (Cindy)
> I saw pumpkins. (Ronald)
> I saw baby animals. (Robert)
> I saw a dog. (Donna)

Materials:

- lined chart paper (preferably manila tagboard)
- magic markers
- white or manila construction paper (usually 12" x 18")
- sentence strips, scissors, glue
- crayons

Procedure:

- The teacher talks about the things children saw at the farm.
- Children dictate their sentences as the teacher writes them on a chart.
- Each child "touch reads" her own sentence on the chart.
- "Sentence builders" focuses on sentences, words, letters, and letter-sounds.
- Sentences on sentence strips are cut apart, glued on construction paper, then illustrated by students to make the pages of a class book.

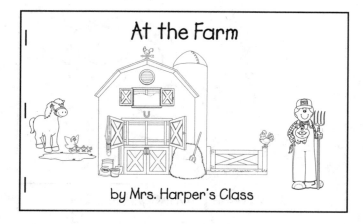

At the Farm
by Mrs. Harper's Class

I saw pumpkins. (Ronald)

At Old Salem*

Some typical responses:

> At Old Salem
> I saw houses. (Mrs. Rolfe)
> I saw candles. (David)
> I saw people in old costumes. (Eleanor)
> I saw an oven. (Susan)
> I saw cookies. (Sally)

*A predictable chart can be completed after visiting any historical site or village.

Materials:

- lined chart paper (preferably manila tagboard)
- magic markers
- white or manila construction paper (usually 12" x 18")
- sentence strips, scissors, glue
- crayons

Procedure:

- The teacher talks about Old Salem and the people and places the students saw.
- Children dictate their sentences as the teacher writes them on a chart.
- Each child "touch reads" his own sentence on the chart.
- "Sentence builders" focuses on sentences, words, letters, and letter-sounds.
- Sentences on sentence strips are cut apart, glued on construction paper, then illustrated by students to make the pages of a class book.

At the School Assembly

Some typical responses:

> At the School Assembly
> I saw the principal. (Mrs. Blackwell)
> I saw the music teacher. (Diane)
> I saw a piano. (Drew)
> I saw children singing. (Chad)
> I saw children dancing. (Pat)

Materials:

- lined chart paper (preferably manila tagboard)
- magic markers
- white or manila construction paper (usually 12" x 18")
- sentence strips, scissors, glue
- crayons

Procedure:

- The teacher talks about the things the class saw at the assembly.
- Children dictate their sentences as the teacher writes them on a chart.
- Each child "touch reads" her own sentence on the chart.
- "Sentence builders" focuses on sentences, words, letters, and letter-sounds.
- Sentences on sentence strips are cut apart, glued on construction paper, then illustrated by students to make the pages of a class book.

At the Grocery Store

Some typical responses:

> At the Grocery Store
> We saw the manager. (Mrs. Hedrick)
> We saw groceries. (Johnny)
> We saw oranges. (Allison)
> We saw cereal boxes. (Greg)
> We saw bananas. (Katherine)

Materials:

- lined chart paper (preferably manila tagboard)
- magic markers
- white or manila construction paper (usually 12" x 18")
- sentence strips, scissors, glue
- crayons

Procedure:

- The teacher talks about the things children saw at the neighborhood grocery store.
- Children dictate their sentences as the teacher writes them on a chart.
- Each child "touch reads" his own sentence on the chart.
- "Sentence builders" focuses on sentences, words, letters, and letter-sounds.
- Sentences on sentence strips are cut apart, glued on construction paper, then illustrated by students to make the pages of a class book.

At the Beach

Some typical responses:

> At the Beach
> You can see the waves. (Mrs. Summers)
> You can see fish. (Mark)
> You can see swimmers. (Laura)
> You can see seagulls. (Ben)
> You can see crabs. (Lonnie)

Materials:

- lined chart paper (preferably manila tagboard)
- magic markers
- white or manila construction paper (usually 12" x 18")
- sentence strips, scissors, glue
- crayons

Procedure:

- The teacher talks about the ocean, waves, what is in the ocean, what is on the beach, etc.
- Children dictate their sentences as the teacher writes them on a chart.
- Each child "touch reads" her own sentence on the chart.
- "Sentence builders" focuses on sentences, words, letters, and letter-sounds.
- Sentences on sentence strips are cut apart, glued on construction paper, then illustrated by students to make the pages of a class book.

At the Science Museum

Some typical responses:

> At the Science Museum
>
> We saw live animals. (Mr. Cashion)
>
> We saw snakes. (Chad)
>
> We saw birds. (Stanley)
>
> We saw a leopard. (Wendy)
>
> We saw the planets. (Michelle)

Materials:

- lined chart paper (preferably manila tagboard)
- magic markers
- white or manila construction paper (usually 12" x 18")
- sentence strips, scissors, glue
- crayons

Procedure:

- The teacher talks about the many things the class saw at the science museum.
- Children dictate their sentences as the teacher writes them on a chart.
- Each child "touch reads" her own sentence on the chart.
- "Sentence builders" focuses on sentences, words, letters, and letter-sounds.
- Sentences on sentence strips are cut apart, glued on construction paper, then illustrated by students to make the pages of a class book.

At the Science Museum

by Mr. Cashion's Class

GRRR!

We saw a leopard. (Wendy)

At the Art Museum

Some typical responses:

> At the Art Museum
> I saw paintings. (Mrs. Williams)
> I saw lots of pictures. (Dick)
> I saw a mother and baby. (Elaine)
> I saw some statues. (Melissa)
> I saw a clay pot. (Laura)

Materials:

- lined chart paper (preferably manila tagboard)
- magic markers
- white or manila construction paper (usually 12" x 18")
- sentence strips, scissors, glue
- crayons

Procedure:

- The teacher talks about the things the children saw at the art museum.
- Children dictate their sentences as the teacher writes them on a chart.
- Each child "touch reads" his own sentence on the chart.
- "Sentence builders" focuses on sentences, words, letters, and letter-sounds.
- Sentences on sentence strips are cut apart, glued on construction paper, then illustrated by students to make the pages of a class book.

I saw a mummy. (Norman)

At the Library

Some typical responses:

> At the Library
> My favorite book is <u>Bats</u>. (Mrs. Gingras)
> My favorite book is <u>Stellaluna</u>. (Karen)
> My favorite book is <u>Curious George</u>. (Genny)
> My favorite book is <u>Rainbow Fish</u>. (Sue)
> My favorite book is <u>Madeline</u>. (Robby)

Materials:

- lined chart paper (preferably manila tagboard)
- magic markers
- white or manila construction paper (usually 12" x 18")
- sentence strips, scissors, glue
- crayons

Procedure:

- The teacher talks about the books the children saw at the local library.
- Children dictate their sentences as the teacher writes them on a chart.
- Each child "touch reads" her own sentence on the chart.
- "Sentence builders" focuses on sentences, words, letters, and letter-sounds.
- Cut apart the sentences on sentence strips, glue on a page, then illustrate.
- Make a class book.

At the Book Fair

Some typical responses:

> At the Book Fair
> My favorite book was <u>Swimmy</u>. (Mr. Rogers)
> My favorite book was <u>Clifford's ABC</u>. (Ray)
> My favorite book was <u>Curious George</u>. (Bob)
> My favorite book was <u>Paddington's ABC</u>. (Nancy)
> My favorite book was <u>Dinosaurs</u>. (Becky)

Materials:

- lined chart paper (preferably manila tagboard)
- magic markers
- white or manila construction paper (usually 12" x 18")
- sentence strips, scissors, glue
- crayons

Procedure:

- The teacher talks about the books and other items available for children at the book fair.
- Children dictate their sentences as the teacher writes them on a chart.
- Each child "touch reads" her own sentence on the chart.
- "Sentence builders" focuses on sentences, words, letters, and letter-sounds.
- Sentences on sentence strips are cut apart, glued on construction paper, then illustrated by students to make the pages of a class book.

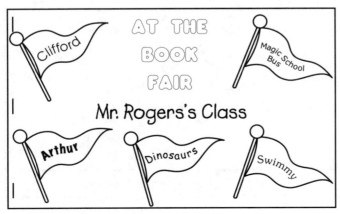

In Fall

Some typical responses:

In Fall
We see colored leaves. (Miss Graham)
We see acorns. (Susan)
We see squirrels. (Thad)
We see haystacks. (Ellen)
We see pumpkins. (Lannie)

Materials:

- lined chart paper (preferably manila tagboard)
- magic markers
- white or manila construction paper (usually 12" x 18")
- sentence strips, scissors, glue
- crayons

Procedure:

- The teacher talks about the things the children see outside in the fall.
- Children dictate their sentences as the teacher writes them on a chart.
- Each child "touch reads" his own sentence on the chart.
- "Sentence builders" focuses on sentences, words, letters, and letter-sounds.
- Sentences on sentence strips are cut apart, glued on construction paper, then illustrated by students to make the pages of a class book.

On Halloween

Some typical responses:

> On Halloween
> I will be a fireman. (Mr. Richardson)
> I will be a princess. (Susanne)
> I will be a cowboy. (Chris)
> I will be a nurse. (Paula)
> I will be a monster. (Gail)

Materials:

- lined chart paper (preferably manila tagboard)
- magic markers
- white or manila construction paper (usually 12" x 18")
- sentence strips, scissors, glue
- crayons

Procedure:

- The teacher talks about the costumes the children will wear on Halloween.
- Children dictate their sentences as the teacher writes them on a chart.
- Each child "touch reads" his own sentence on the chart.
- "Sentence builders" focuses on sentences, words, letters, and letter-sounds.
- Sentences on sentence strips are cut apart, glued on construction paper, then illustrated by students to make the pages of a class book.

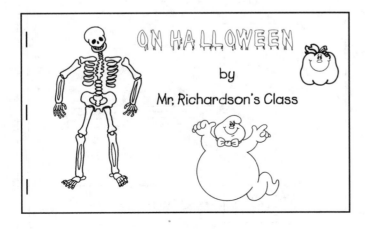

Thanksgiving

Some typical responses:

> Thanksgiving
> I am thankful for a good class. (Mrs. Kump)
> I am thankful for good food. (Bob)
> I am thankful for friends. (Bobby)
> I am thankful for horses. (Kathy)
> I am thankful for books. (Laura)

Materials:

- lined chart paper (preferably manila tagboard)
- magic markers
- white or manila construction paper (usually 12" x 18")
- sentence strips, scissors, glue
- crayons

Procedure:

- The teacher talks about Thanksgiving and all the things for which the children are thankful.
- Children dictate their sentences as the teacher writes them on a chart.
- Each child "touch reads" her own sentence on the chart.
- "Sentence builders" focuses on sentences, words, letters, and letter-sounds.
- Sentences on sentence strips are cut apart, glued on construction paper, then illustrated by students to make the pages of a class book.

New Year's Resolutions

Some typical responses:

> New Year's Resolutions
> I will walk every day. (Miss Wellman)
> I will be good. (Summer)
> I will help my mother. (Emily)
> I will clean my room. (Scott)
> I will not eat junk food. (Jamie)

Materials:

- lined chart paper (preferably manila tagboard)
- magic markers
- white or manila construction paper (usually 12" x 18")
- sentence strips, scissors, glue
- crayons

Procedure:

- The teacher talks about New Year's resolutions and what the children want to change.
- Children dictate their sentences as the teacher writes them on a chart.
- Each child "touch reads" his own sentence on the chart.
- "Sentence builders" focuses on sentences, words, letters, and letter-sounds.
- Sentences on sentence strips are cut apart, glued on construction paper, then illustrated by students to make the pages of a class book.

In Winter

Some typical responses:

> In Winter
> I will wear a warm coat. (Mrs. Sigmon)
> I will make a snowman. (Caroline)
> I will play in the snow. (Ray)
> I will make snow cream. (Ashley)
> I will go skiing. (Blake)

Materials:

- lined chart paper (preferably manila tagboard)
- magic markers
- white or manila construction paper (usually 12" x 18")
- sentence strips, scissors, glue
- crayons

Procedure:

- The teacher talks about the things people can do in the snow/winter.
- Children dictate their sentences as the teacher writes them on a chart.
- Each child "touch reads" her own sentence on the chart.
- "Sentence builders" focuses on sentences, words, letters, and letter-sounds.
- Sentences on sentence strips are cut apart, glued on construction paper, then illustrated by students to make the pages of a class book.

In Winter

Mrs. Sigmon's Class

I will go skiing. (Blake)

Martin Luther King, Jr.'s Birthday

Some typical responses:

> I Have a Dream
>
> I have a dream that there will be peace. (Miss Wishon)
>
> I have a dream that everyone will get along. (Jim)
>
> I have a dream that there is no war. (Ashley)
>
> I have a dream that people will help each other. (Ben)
>
> I have a dream that everyone loves each other. (Mark)

Materials:

- lined chart paper (preferably manila tagboard)
- magic markers
- white or manila construction paper (usually 12" x 18")
- sentence strips, scissors, glue
- crayons

Procedure:

- The teacher talks or reads about Martin Luther King, Jr. and his dream.
- Children dictate their sentences as the teacher writes them on a chart.
- Each child "touch reads" his own sentence on the chart.
- "Sentence builders" focuses on sentences, words, letters, and letter-sounds.
- Sentences on sentence strips are cut apart, glued on construction paper, then illustrated by students to make the pages of a class book.

100th Day of School

Some typical responses:

> 100th Day of School
> I brought 100 pennies. (Mr. Wilkes)
> I brought 100 Cheerios*. (Jamie)
> I brought 100 buttons. (Judy)
> I brought 100 raisins. (Thad)
> I brought 100 marbles. (Quinton)

*Cheerios is a registered trademark of General Mills, Inc.

Materials:

- lined chart paper (preferably manila tagboard)
- magic markers
- white or manila construction paper (usually 12" x 18")
- sentence strips, scissors, glue
- crayons

Procedure:

- The teacher talks about what the children brought to school to celebrate the 100th day.
- Children dictate their sentences as the teacher writes them on a chart.
- Each child "touch reads" his own sentence on the chart.
- "Sentence builders" focuses on sentences, words, letters, and letter-sounds.
- Sentences on sentence strips are cut apart, glued on construction paper, then illustrated by students to make the pages of a class book.

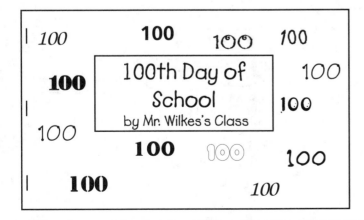

Valentine's Day

Some typical responses:

> Valentine's Day
> I love my family. (Mr. Smith)
> I love books. (Deb)
> I love computers. (David)
> I love all my friends at school. (Lauren)
> I love my brothers and sisters. (Laura)

Materials:

- lined chart paper (preferably manila tagboard)
- magic markers
- white or manila construction paper (usually 12" x 18")
- sentence strips, scissors, glue
- crayons

Procedure:

- The teacher talks about Valentine's Day and all the things the children "love."
- Children dictate their sentences as the teacher writes them on a chart.
- Each child "touch reads" his own sentence on the chart.
- "Sentence builders" focuses on sentences, words, letters, and letter-sounds.
- Sentences on sentence strips are cut apart, glued on construction paper, then illustrated by students to make the pages of a class book.

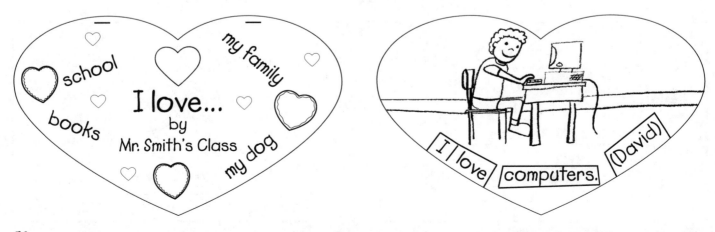

In Spring

Some typical responses:

> In Spring
> I like to walk outside. (Mrs. Tillman)
> I like to plant flowers. (Cece)
> I like to swing on my swing. (Vicky)
> I like to play t-ball. (Joshua)
> I like to play soccer. (Alex)

Materials:

- lined chart paper (preferably manila tagboard)
- magic markers
- white or manila construction paper (usually 12" x 18")
- sentence strips, scissors, glue
- crayons

Procedure:

- The teacher talks about the activities the children can do outside in the nice spring weather.
- Children dictate their sentences as the teacher writes them on a chart.
- Each child "touch reads" her own sentence on the chart.
- "Sentence builders" focuses on sentences, words, letters, and letter-sounds.
- Sentences on sentence strips are cut apart, glued on construction paper, then illustrated by students to make the pages of a class book.

I like to swing on my swing. (Vicky)

The End of the School Year

Some typical responses:

> The End of the School Year
> At school I learned to read. (Mr. Weber)
> At school I learned to count. (Brent)
> At school I learned to estimate. (Vickie)
> At school I learned to write. (Alex)
> At school I learned to sing. (Whitney)

Materials:

- lined chart paper (preferably manila tagboard)
- magic markers
- white or manila construction paper (usually 12" x 18")
- sentence strips, scissors, glue
- crayons

Procedure:

- The teacher talks about the things the children learned to do this year in school.
- Children dictate their sentences as the teacher writes them on a chart.
- Each child "touch reads" his own sentence on the chart.
- "Sentence builders" focuses on sentences, words, letters, and letter-sounds.
- Sentences on sentence strips are cut apart, glued on construction paper, then illustrated by students to make the pages of a class book.

Friends

Some typical responses:

> Friends
> My friend is Pat. (Mrs. Moore)
> My friend is Sharon. (Arthur)
> My friend is Jim. (David)
> My friend is Chris. (John)
> My friend is Joey. (Kevin)

Materials:

- lined chart paper (preferably manila tagboard)
- magic markers
- white or manila construction paper (usually 12" x 18")
- sentence strips, scissors, glue
- crayons

Procedure:

- The teacher talks about friends and friendships.
- Children dictate their sentences as the teacher writes them on a chart.
- Each child "touch reads" her own sentence on the chart.
- "Sentence builders" focuses on sentences, words, letters, and letter-sounds.
- Sentences on sentence strips are cut apart, glued on construction paper, then illustrated by students to make the pages of a class book.

Plants

Some typical responses:

Plants
I will plant flowers. (Ms. Cunningham)
I will plant marigolds. (William)
I will plant azaleas. (Joyce)
I will plant beans. (Carol)
I will plant tomatoes. (Bobby)

Materials:

- lined chart paper (preferably manila tagboard)
- magic markers
- white or manila construction paper (usually 12" x 18")
- sentence strips, scissors, glue
- crayons

Procedure:

- Talk about what people plant in gardens (vegetables, flowers, etc.).
- Children dictate their sentences as the teacher writes them on a chart.
- Each child "touch reads" her own sentence on the chart.
- "Sentence builders" focuses on sentences, words, letters, and letter-sounds.
- Sentences on sentence strips are cut apart, glued on construction paper, then illustrated by students to make the pages of a class book.

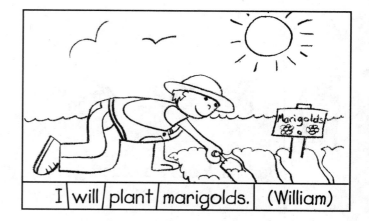

Family

Some typical responses:

> Family
> My family likes to read books. (Mrs. Marr)
> My family likes to eat together. (David)
> My family likes to go to church. (James)
> My family likes to go for a ride. (Anne)
> My family likes to work together. (Lisa)

Materials:

- lined chart paper (preferably manila tagboard)
- magic markers
- white or manila construction paper (usually 12" x 18")
- sentence strips, scissors, glue
- crayons

Procedure:

- The teacher talks about families and all the activities they do together.
- Children dictate their sentences as the teacher writes them on a chart.
- Each child "touch reads" his own sentence on the chart.
- "Sentence builders" focuses on sentences, words, letters, and letter-sounds.
- Sentences on sentence strips are cut apart, glued on construction paper, then illustrated by students to make the pages of a class book.

The Wind

Some typical responses:

> The Wind
> The wind blew *my* clothes. (Ms. Sykes)
> The wind blew *my* kite. (Brenda)
> The wind blew *my* hair. (Laurie)
> The wind blew the trees. (Wayne)
> The wind blew the *umbrella*. (Susan)

Materials:

- lined chart paper (preferably manila tagboard)
- magic markers
- white or manila construction paper (usually 12" x 18")
- sentence strips, scissors, glue
- crayons

Procedure:

- The teacher talks about the wind and all the things the wind can blow.
- Children dictate their sentences as the teacher writes them on a chart.
- Each child "touch reads" her own sentence on the chart.
- "Sentence builders" focuses on sentences, words, letters, and letter-sounds.
- Sentences on sentence strips are cut apart, glued on construction paper, then illustrated by students to make the pages of a class book.

Water

Some typical responses:

> ### Water
> I use water to drink. (Mrs. Johnson)
> I use water to wash dishes. (Daisy)
> I use water to water the grass. (Chuck)
> I use water to brush my teeth. (Gabrielle)
> I use water to wash the car. (Jimmy)

Materials:

- lined chart paper (preferably manila tagboard)
- magic markers
- white or manila construction paper (usually 12" x 18")
- sentence strips, scissors, glue
- crayons

Procedure:

- The teacher talks about the things people do with water, especially young children.
- Children dictate their sentences as the teacher writes them on a chart.
- Each child "touch reads" his own sentence on the chart.
- "Sentence builders" focuses on sentences, words, letters, and letter-sounds.
- Sentences on sentence strips are cut apart, glued on construction paper, then illustrated by students to make the pages of a class book.

Pets

Some typical responses:

Pets
My favorite pet is a cat. (Mrs. Joyner)
My favorite pet is a hamster. (David)
My favorite pet is a bird. (Ashley)
My favorite pet is a pony. (Ben)
My favorite pet is a dog. (Jake)

Materials:

- lined chart paper (preferably manila tagboard)
- magic markers
- white or manila construction paper (usually 12" x 18")
- sentence strips, scissors, glue
- crayons

Procedure:

- The teacher talks about pets: What makes a good pet? What are a pet owner's responsibilities?
- Children dictate their sentences as the teacher writes them on a chart.
- Each child "touch reads" her own sentence on the chart.
- "Sentence builders" focuses on sentences, words, letters, and letter-sounds.
- Sentences on sentence strips are cut apart, glued on construction paper, then illustrated by students to make the pages of a class book.

Bears

Some typical responses:

> Bears
> Bears are animals. (Mrs. Poholsky)
> Bears are toys. (John)
> Bears are in the zoo. (Susan)
> Bears are big. (Abby)
> Bears are little. (Alex)

Materials:

- lined chart paper (preferably manila tagboard)
- magic markers
- white or manila construction paper (usually 12" x 18")
- sentence strips, scissors, glue
- crayons

Procedure:

- The teacher talks about bears—real bears in the wild and in zoos, as well as teddy bears.
- Children dictate their sentences as the teacher writes them on a chart.
- Each child "touch reads" her own sentence on the chart.
- "Sentence builders" focuses on sentences, words, letters, and letter-sounds.
- Sentences on sentence strips are cut apart, glued on construction paper, then illustrated by students to make the pages of a class book.

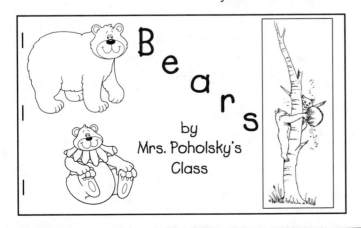

School

Some typical responses:

> School
> In school I like to read. (Mr. Parker)
> In school I like to write. (Jackie)
> In school I like to do the calendar. (Vincent)
> In school I like to learn. (Janice)
> In school I like centers. (Benjamin)

Materials:

- lined chart paper (preferably manila tagboard)
- magic markers
- white or manila construction paper (usually 12" x 18")
- sentence strips, scissors, glue
- crayons

Procedure:

- The teacher talks about all the things students do in school each day.
- Children dictate their sentences as the teacher writes them on a chart.
- Each child "touch reads" his own sentence on the chart.
- "Sentence builders" focuses on sentences, words, letters, and letter-sounds.
- Sentences on sentence strips are cut apart, glued on construction paper, then illustrated by students to make the pages of a class book.

Weather

Some typical responses:

> Weather
> The weather can be sunny. (Mrs. Reynolds)
> The weather can be rainy. (Jaquaine)
> The weather can be hot. (Adrienne)
> The weather can be cold. (Jade)
> The weather can be windy. (Cayenne)

Materials:

- lined chart paper (preferably manila tagboard)
- magic markers
- white or manila construction paper (usually 12" x 18")
- sentence strips, scissors, glue
- crayons

Procedure:

- The teacher talks about the weather (changes, patterns, temperatures, etc.).
- Children dictate their sentences as the teacher writes them on a chart.
- Each child "touch reads" her own sentence on the chart.
- "Sentence builders" focuses on sentences, words, letters, and letter-sounds.
- Sentences on sentence strips are cut apart, glued on construction paper, then illustrated by students to make the pages of a class book.

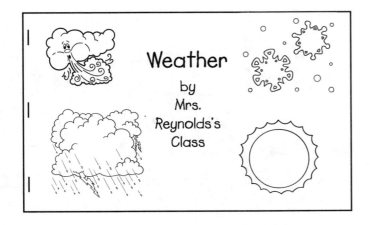

The | weather | can | be | cold. | (Jade)

Living and Nonliving

Some typical responses:

> Living and Nonliving
> A person is living. (Mrs. Hall)
> A plant is living. (Charles)
> A cat is living. (Britta)
> A car is nonliving. (Hoyt)
> A rock is nonliving. (Kendra)

Materials:

- lined chart paper (preferably manila tagboard)
- magic markers
- white or manila construction paper (usually 12" x 18")
- sentence strips, scissors, glue
- crayons

Procedure:

- The teacher talks about things that are living and nonliving.
- Children dictate their sentences as the teacher writes them on a chart.
- Each child "touch reads" her own sentence on the chart.
- "Sentence builders" focuses on sentences, words, letters, and letter-sounds.
- Sentences on sentence strips are cut apart, glued on construction paper, then illustrated by students to make the pages of a class book.

If I Was a Kite

Some typical responses:

> If I Was a Kite
> I would fly to Arizona. (Mrs. Tysinger)
> I would fly to the park. (Allie)
> I would fly to New York. (Jonathan)
> I would fly to school. (Blair Macy)
> I would fly to my old house. (Bret)

Materials:

- lined chart paper (preferably manila tagboard)
- magic markers
- white or manila construction paper (usually 12" x 18")
- sentence strips, scissors, glue
- crayons

Procedure:

- The teacher talks about kites and places the students could fly.
- Children dictate their sentences as the teacher writes them on a chart.
- Each child "touch reads" his own sentence on the chart.
- "Sentence builders" focuses on sentences, words, letters, and letter-sounds.
- Sentences on sentence strips are cut apart, glued on construction paper, then illustrated by students to make the pages of a class book.

If I Had a Pet

Some typical responses:

> If I Had a Pet
> I would have to feed it. (Mrs. West)
> I would have to find it a place to sleep. (Taylor)
> I would have to give it a bath. (Gray)
> I would have to play with it. (Paul)
> I would have to take it to the vet. (Gregory)

Materials:
- lined chart paper (preferably manila tagboard)
- magic markers
- white or manila construction paper (usually 12" x 18")
- sentence strips, scissors, glue
- crayons

Procedure:
- The teacher talks about the kinds of pets people have and how they care for their pets.
- Children dictate their sentences as the teacher writes them on a chart.
- Each child "touch reads" his own sentence on the chart.
- "Sentence builders" focuses on sentences, words, letters, and letter-sounds.
- Sentences on sentence strips are cut apart, glued on construction paper, then illustrated by students to make the pages of a class book.

If I Had a Garden

Some typical responses:

> If I Had a Garden
> I would plant seeds. (Mrs. Davis)
> I would water it. (Kearns)
> I would weed it. (Ward)
> I would plant lots of flowers. (Joanna)
> I would grow vegetables. (Bill)

Materials:

- lined chart paper (preferably manila tagboard)
- magic markers
- white or manila construction paper (usually 12" x 18")
- sentence strips, scissors, glue
- crayons

Procedure:

- The teacher talks about how people plant and take care of gardens.
- Children dictate their sentences as the teacher writes them on a chart.
- Each child "touch reads" her own sentence on the chart.
- "Sentence builders" focuses on sentences, words, letters, and letter-sounds.
- Sentences on sentence strips are cut apart, glued on construction paper, then illustrated by students to make the pages of a class book.

If I Went to a Restaurant

Some typical responses:

> If I Went to a Restaurant
> I would eat tacos. (Mrs. Keith)
> I would eat enchiladas. (Kay)
> I would eat salsa and chips. (Norma)
> I would eat tamales. (Manuel)
> I would eat burritos. (José)

Materials:

- lined chart paper (preferably manila tagboard)
- magic markers
- white or manila construction paper (usually 12" x 18")
- sentence strips, scissors, glue
- crayons

Procedure:

- The teacher talks about the kinds of food people eat at a restaurant.
- Children dictate their sentences as the teacher writes them on a chart.
- Each child "touch reads" his own sentence on the chart.
- "Sentence builders" focuses on sentences, words, letters, and letter-sounds.
- Sentences on sentence strips are cut apart, glued on construction paper, then illustrated by students to make the pages of a class book.

If I Could Cook

Some typical responses:

> If I Could Cook
> I would make cookies. (Mrs. Peller)
> I would make cookies. (Josh)
> I would make blueberry muffins. (Jacob)
> I would make hamburgers. (Jeremy)
> I would make spaghetti. (Virginia)

Materials:

- lined chart paper (preferably manila tagboard)
- magic markers
- white or manila construction paper (usually 12" x 18")
- sentence strips, scissors, glue
- crayons

Procedure:

- The teacher talks about cooking: What can you cook? What can you make?
- Children dictate their sentences as the teacher writes them on a chart.
- Each child "touch reads" her own sentence on the chart.
- "Sentence builders" focuses on sentences, words, letters, and letter-sounds.
- Sentences on sentence strips are cut apart, glued on construction paper, then illustrated by students to make the pages of a class book.

If I Could Cook by Mrs. Peller's Class

I would make hamburgers. (Jeremy)

If I Could Pick a Song

Some typical responses:

> If I Could Pick a Song
> I would sing, "America." (Mrs. Carroll)
> I would sing, "The Wheels on the Bus." (Carol)
> I would sing, " Yankee Doodle." (Linda)
> I would sing, "Good Morning to You." (Janie)
> I would sing, "This Old Man." (Scott)

Materials:

- lined chart paper (preferably manila tagboard)
- magic markers
- white or manila construction paper (usually 12" x 18")
- sentence strips, scissors, glue
- crayons

Procedure:

- The teacher talks about the songs we sing in school (in our classroom, at music class, etc.).
- Children dictate their sentences as the teacher writes them on a chart.
- Each child "touch reads" his own sentence on the chart.
- "Sentence builders" focuses on sentences, words, letters, and letter-sounds.
- Sentences on sentence strips are cut apart, glued on construction paper, then illustrated by students to make the pages of a class book.

If I Could Get a Book

Some typical responses:

> If I Could Get a Book
> I would pick The Three Bears. (Ms. Soles)
> I would pick The Gingerbread Man. (Jan)
> I would pick The Mitten. (Jonathan)
> I would pick The Magic School Bus Inside
> the Earth. (Abby)
> I would pick Ira Sleeps Over. (Alex)

Materials:

- lined chart paper (preferably manila tagboard)
- magic markers
- white or manila construction paper (usually 12" x 18")
- sentence strips, scissors, glue
- crayons

Procedure:

- The teacher talks about the children's favorite books, including what books they choose in the book center, at the library, at the book fair, or at a book store.
- Children dictate their sentences as the teacher writes them on a chart.
- Each child "touch reads" his own sentence on the chart.
- "Sentence builders" focuses on sentences, words, letters, and letter-sounds.
- Sentences on sentence strips are cut apart, glued on construction paper, then illustrated by students to make the pages of a class book.

If I Am Thirsty I Drink

Some typical responses:

> If I Am Thirsty I Drink
> I drink water. (Miss Shinn)
> I drink orange juice. (Mary Hannah)
> I drink lemonade. (Lowell)
> I drink water. (John)
> I drink apple juice. (Paul)

Materials:

- lined chart paper (preferably manila tagboard)
- magic markers
- white or manila construction paper (usually 12" x 18")
- sentence strips, scissors, glue
- crayons

Procedure:

- Talk about all the liquids people drink when they are thirsty, emphasizing those that are healthy.
- Children dictate their sentences as the teacher writes them on a chart.
- Each child "touch reads" her own sentence on the chart.
- "Sentence builders" focuses on sentences, words, letters, and letter-sounds.
- Sentences on sentence strips are cut apart, glued on construction paper, then illustrated by students to make the pages of a class book.

I Will Take Care of the Earth

Some typical responses:

> I Will Take Care of the Earth
> I will plant a tree. (Mrs. Spencer)
> I will pick up trash. (DeLinda)
> I will not throw trash. (Tammie)
> I will not cut down trees. (Mario)
> I will not kill animals. (Angie H.)

Materials:

- lined chart paper (preferably manila tagboard)
- magic markers
- white or manila construction paper (usually 12" x 18")
- sentence strips, scissors, glue
- crayons

Procedure:

- The teacher talks about the things people can do to take care of the Earth.
- Children dictate their sentences as the teacher writes them on a chart.
- Each child "touch reads" his own sentence on the chart.
- "Sentence builders" focuses on sentences, words, letters, and letter-sounds.
- Sentences on sentence strips are cut apart, glued on construction paper, then illustrated by students to make the pages of a class book.

Sports

Some typical responses:

> Sports
> My favorite sport is basketball. (Mrs. Hall)
> My favorite sport is soccer. (Sarah)
> My favorite sport is swimming. (Alex)
> My favorite sport is baseball. (Joannie)
> My favorite sport is gymnastics. (Dennis)

Materials:

- lined chart paper (preferably manila tagboard)
- magic markers
- white or manila construction paper (usually 12" x 18")
- sentence strips, scissors, glue
- crayons

Procedure:

- The teacher talks about the students' favorite sports to watch and play.
- Children dictate their sentences as the teacher writes them on a chart.
- Each child "touch reads" his own sentence on the chart.
- "Sentence builders" focuses on sentences, words, letters, and letter-sounds.
- Sentences on sentence strips are cut apart, glued on construction paper, then illustrated by students to make the pages of a class book.

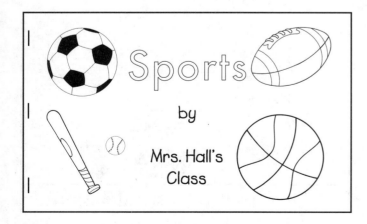